The
ARROWS
of the
LORD

Inkwell Heritage Publishing
18896 Greenwell Springs Road
Greenwell Springs, LA 70739

The
ARROWS
of the
LORD

by

Andrea "Andy" McDougal

Published by:

Inkwell Heritage Publishing
18896 Greenwell Springs Road
Greenwell Springs, LA 70739

ISBN 989-8-9987460-3-1

Printed on demand in the US, the UK and Australia
For Worldwide Distribution

The LORD has called me from the womb; from the body of my mother He has named my name. And He has made my mouth like a sharp sword; in the shadow of His hand has He hid me and made me a polished arrow; in His quiver has He kept me close and concealed me.

Isaiah 49:1-2

Acknowledgments

Many thanks to Marilyn McDaniel for her faithfulness in transcribing the messages that make up this book.

Your arrows are sharp; the peoples fall under You;
Your darts pierce the hearts of the King's enemies.
Psalm 45:5

Other Books by Andy McDougal

The Glory of God Revealed

His Wonders in the Deep

Understanding the Seed

YOUR Camels Are Coming

The Power of the Seed

Contents

arrow

Pronounced erō, noun, plural *arrows*: "a shaft sharpened at the front and with feathers or vanes at the back, shot from a bow as a weapon or for sport: 'his ability to launch an arrow accurately.' " Synonyms: shaft, bolt, dart.

quiver

"A container for holding arrows, bolts, or darts. It could be carried on an archer's body, the bow, or the ground, depending on the type of shooting and the archer's personal preference."

Arrows in God's Quiver

But no weapon that is formed against you shall prosper, and every tongue that shall rise against you in judgment you shall show to be in the wrong. This [peace, righteousness, security, triumph over opposition] is the heritage of the servants of the Lord [those in whom the ideal Servant of the Lord is reproduced]; this is the righteousness or the vindication which they obtain from Me [this is that which I impart to them as their justification], says the Lord.

Isaiah 54:17

There is an anointing in us to break the yoke of every enemy that comes against us and tries to overtake us. God said it Himself. No weapon that is formed against us will ever be able to prosper. Why? Because of the anointing of the Most High God, the Holy Spirit that is on the inside of each of us.

There will be weapons formed against us, and, at times, you will see them being formed, but they will never prosper. We have weapons of our own, and we are weapons ourselves. The Word of God has much to say about the arrows of the Lord. We will look at these teachings so that we can learn from them.

You are an arrow of the Lord in His hands, and He will give you the arrows of His Word to tear down every enemy. I am not speaking of weapons to fight flesh and blood, but rather weapons to fight against our spiritual enemies. If God uses you to preach His Word, you are sending forth the arrows of the Lord, and they should be hitting the desired target.

If you have arrows, you need something to carry them in, something to contain them, and it is called a quiver. The Bible tells us that we are the arrows in God's quiver, and that is the subject of this first chapter. It is personal, for you. *You* are an arrow in God's quiver.

In the natural, arrows are very powerful weapons, and the arrows of God found in His Word are no less powerful. We just need to recognize that we have them and to learn to use them well.

Our children are a blessing, the Scriptures show:

YOU ARE AN ARROW OF
THE LORD IN HIS HANDS,
AND HE WILL GIVE YOU
THE ARROWS OF HIS
WORD TO TEAR DOWN
EVERY ENEMY!

Behold, children are a heritage from the LORD, the fruit of the womb a reward. As arrows are in the hand of a warrior, so are the children of one's youth. Happy, blessed, and fortunate is the man whose quiver is filled with them! They will not be put to shame when they speak with their adversaries [in gatherings] at the [city's] gate.

Psalm 127:3-5

Notice several important things in this passage. First, arrows are to be found in the hands of a warrior. If you are a child of God, the arrows of God have been granted unto you, and that qualifies you as a warrior in His Kingdom. Rise up therefore and fight.

The second thing to notice here is this: *"blessed, and fortunate is the man whose quiver is filled with them!"* In this context, it is talking about our children, but in a larger context it is telling us that we are blessed if our quiver is full of the arrows of the Lord. The promise is: *"They will not be put to shame when they speak with their adversaries in gatherings at the city's gate."* How wonderful!

Again, in the narrower context, this speaks of a mother and father, but in the larger context it speaks of those who go up against their enemies at the gates. And that's exactly what we need to do.

In ancient times, many things took place at the gates of a city. It was a place of commerce and communication, and it was a place where the elders of the city met to make serious decisions relating to the common welfare of all the citizens. It was also the place where enemies were confronted, and, if possible, repelled. In our case, we are talking about spiritual gates, and the promise is that we will be victorious when we come up against our enemies at the gates.

Isaiah 28:6 shows us that we are to push back or stop the enemy *"at the gate."* There are many spiritual gates that surround us, and those of us who have our quiver full will be able to overcome all potential intruders.

Before we get to the subject of a husband and a wife having their quiver full of children, let me state this: If your quiver is full of arrows, when you go up to deal with an enemy at any gate, you will be successful. You might be walking through to the other side of something, and you come to a spiritual gate. You may be stepping out into your ministry, and suddenly you come up against a wall in the Spirit realm. That is an enemy you need to deal with. When you come up to any gate, if you have a quiver full of arrows, you will defeat your enemies. That is God's

THE ENEMY WILL
INVARIABLY COME UP
AGAINST YOU, AND
WHEN HE DOES, YOU
MUST BE READY!

promise, and it is a powerful one. You will defeat your enemies!

Again, the gates of those ancient cities were important. It was there that they settled governmental and judgmental issues. But your gates are just as important. The enemy will invariably come up against you, and when he does, you must be ready. When you are going through a gate of ministry, a gate of worship or a gate of prosperity and blessing, and the enemy tries to stop the move of God in your life, you can have a quiver full of arrows ready to deal with him. And, if you do, you will be able to destroy each and every enemy that comes up against you. What could be more wonderful?

Job spoke of the arrows of the Lord:

[The arrow] is drawn forth and it comes out after passing through his body; yes, the glittering point comes out of his gall. Terrors march in upon him; every misfortune is laid up for his treasures. A fire not blown by man shall devour him; it shall consume what is left in his tent [and it shall go ill with him who remains there]. The heavens shall reveal his iniquity, and the earth shall rise up against him.

Job 20:25-27

Here we see the effects of the arrows of the Lord. Who does this passage refer to? For us, it is describing what will happen to our enemy when we have the proper arrows in place to defeat him. Again, we are not talking about physical enemies. We are not battling physical enemies, enemies of flesh and blood. These enemies are ruling powers, despotisms in high places. When you choose an arrow from your quiver and place it into your bow—whether it is through intercession or through praise and worship—suddenly the string on that bow is pulled back, and that arrow shoots out and into the very heart of your enemy. That is victory.

It's interesting that this passage mentions the glittering point that comes out of his gall and the terror that marches in upon him as a result. This is a powerful arrow with a deadly point on it, and it is yours to use.

It was prophetically spoken over me that the point or spear of the arrow would be a glittering one. The arrow in this passage did not have a narrow point like some modern metal-tipped arrows do. The older type of arrows, ones used by the Native American Indians, for instance, had a head that was more like the point of a spear.

This one had a glittering point, and when you go up against your spiritual enemies, and you pull

WE ARE NOT TALKING ABOUT PHYSICAL ENEMIES. WE ARE NOT BATTLING PHYSICAL ENEMIES, ENEMIES OF FLESH AND BLOOD. THESE ENEMIES ARE RULING POWERS, DESPOTISMS IN HIGH PLACES!

that arrow out of your quiver, put it in your bow and shoot it, the result will be utter annihilation of the enemy. The arrows God will give you to use are glittering, but they are also deadly:

> *Your arrows are sharp; the peoples fall under You;*
> *Your darts pierce the hearts of the King's enemies.* Psalm 45:5

The fact that the pronouns *You* and *Your* are capitalized here shows us that this passage prophetically referred to Jesus. But you and I, as God's children, have the same promises. Our God is King, and we work to destroy His enemies, for they are our enemies as well.

It works the other way around too. If you have a spiritual enemy, that enemy is also an enemy of God. That enemy hates you because he hated God first, and God is in you. Take an arrow out of your quiver, place it in your bow, and begin to pull on that string. You are about to destroy an enemy of the King and do a service to His Kingdom.

Isaiah prophesied:

> *Listen to me, O isles and coastlands, and hearken, you peoples from afar. The LORD has called*

me from the womb; from the body of my mother He has named my name. And He has made my mouth like a sharp sword; in the shadow of His hand has He hid me and made me a polished arrow; in His quiver has He kept me close and concealed me. Isaiah 49:1-2

Before you ever appeared in your mother's womb, God chose you to be part of His Body and part of His great army. You were actually called before the foundations of the Earth were laid. God not only called you; He also specifically named you. He has also placed a weapon in your mouth and kept you as a polished arrow in His quiver.

Most of us have a spiritual significance to our names, and this shows that we were called by God for a definite purpose in the Earth. You may not have known it, but you were called before you were in your mother's womb. Even then, God had already chosen your name.

He has made my mouth like a sharp sword; in the shadow of His hand has He hid me and made me a polished arrow; in His quiver has He kept me close and concealed me.

Wow! That's powerful, comforting and beautiful!

WHEN GOD MADE HIS COVENANT WITH ABRAHAM, IT THEN FLOWED FROM HIM TO HIS SON ISAAC AND ON TO HIS GRANDSON JACOB, SO THAT OUT OF THEIR SEED CAME THE TWELVE TRIBES OF ISRAEL!

Jeremiah prophesied:

> *For behold, I will raise and cause to come up against Babylon an assembly of great nations from the north country. They will equip and set themselves against her; from there she will be taken. Their arrows will be like [both] an expert, mighty warrior and like his arrows—none [of them] will return in vain.* Jeremiah 50:9

I need to provide a little background here so that we can all understand what was happening with Jeremiah. We must go all the way back to Abraham, Isaac and Jacob. God chose to make a covenant with these men and their descendants.

When God made His covenant with Abraham, it then flowed from him to his son Isaac and on to his grandson Jacob, so that out of their seed came the twelve tribes of Israel. We know that they went into Egypt during a time of famine, and there they found their brother Joseph who had risen to be something like an assistant or viceroy to the king or pharaoh. Amazingly, although Joseph was a Hebrew, he was now the next in the line of authority under Pharaoh. Because of Joseph, the other Hebrew sons of Jacob found favor in Egypt and were able to survive and thrive there during that great time of famine and beyond.

Over time, however, things changed. Several Pharaohs died and were replaced, and the political and social climate in Egypt also changed. With these changes, everything also changed for the people of God. Until this time, the original group that had traveled to Egypt had prospered and grown until they now numbered in the millions. But they were no longer prospering. They had now been enslaved and were living a life of cruel bondage. Things hadn't started out that way, but that was how they ended up.

After many generations, God, through Moses, Aaron and Joshua, released the children of Israel from their bondage, and they were able to cross over and eventually re-enter their Promised Land. There, however, instead of living a life of thanksgiving to the God who had delivered them and blessed them again, the people quickly fell into apostasy, disobeying God and dividing into two kingdoms. Israel, to the north, was a wicked kingdom, and Judah, to the south, was a more righteous kingdom.

When the people sinned, God raised up prophets to speak to them about their sin. Jeremiah was one of those prophets. Through Jeremiah, the Lord

THE ORIGINAL GROUP
THAT HAD TRAVELED TO
EGYPT HAD PROSPERED
AND GROWN UNTIL THEY
NOW NUMBERED IN THE
MILLIONS!

foretold of the coming destruction of Israel and the carrying away of her people into Babylon. This was hard for the Israelites to believe. But, just as God had said, it happened, and they soon found themselves captives again, this time in Babylon.

Now, with that background, lets look at Jeremiah 50:9 again:

For behold, I will raise and cause to come up against Babylon an assembly of great nations from the north country. They will equip and set themselves against her; from there she will be taken. Their arrows will be like [both] an expert, mighty warrior and like his arrows—none [of them] will return in vain.   Jeremiah 50:9

God was about to loose the Israelites out of their captivity, and there are plenty of people alive today who are in spiritual captivity. But we are even now coming into a move of the Spirit of God in which those who are in captivity are coming out. If you are reading this and you are in captivity, right now I command you to come out of your captivity in Jesus' name! He paid the price for your freedom.

God said through Jeremiah that He was raising up those who would come against Babylon, *"an assembly of a great nation from the north country."* These, He said, would *"equip and set themselves against her"* and *"she will be taken."* God is about to destroy all that has caused His twenty-first century people to be in captivity. His arrows have been sent forth in the Earth to destroy the spirit that is holding His people captive.

He also said, *"Their arrows will be like an expert."* He was talking about His archers. Could that include you? Yes, it should. You and I are the archers who are called to shoot forth the Word of God, and when those arrows are shot, God has said: *"none [of them] will return in vain."* Oh, I like that!

Equip yourself and set yourself against spiritual Babylon, and *"she will be taken." Babylon* means "confusion" and refers to the world system and the spirit of religion. That spirit of confusion that has done so much harm is about to come down because of this current move of God.

You and I are just average people, but God said that our arrows will be *"like an expert"* and the promise is that *"none of them will return in vain."* You need to get this because something is happening right now. God is offering you a quiver, and one by one He will add to your arrows, so that when you speak the Word of God, your arrows

YOU ARE A MIGHTY WARRIOR, AND GOD HAS GIVEN YOU A QUIVER FULL OF ARROWS. HE HAS CONFIDENCE IN YOU, SO YOU NEED TO HAVE CONFIDENCE IN YOUR ABILITY THROUGH HIM!

will hit the target every time and do some serious damage to every enemy.

When these archers come up against this enemy, God said, they will prevail. Against what enemies? These include the enemies of the Church, the enemies of the Kingdom, and they include the spiritual enemies that hover over our cities and communities to control them. These are spiritual entities, but God has said that with His arrows shot from our bows, they will come down.

Right now, take an arrow from your quiver, place it into your bow, and aim and shoot. God has said that your arrows will be *like that of an expert mighty warrior.*

Is that possible? Yes, you are a mighty warrior, and God has given you a quiver full of arrows. He has confidence in you, so you need to have confidence in your ability through Him. You will be able to identify the opportune moment. You will be able to select just the right arrow. You will be able to launch it against the enemy. And you will annihilate or destroy that enemy—all in the powerful name of Jesus.

You will not miss the target, for you are a mighty warrior, an expert at warfare with the arrows of the Lord. Not one of those arrows will be shot in vain.

You need to take this word and hide it in your heart. God says that when you shoot His Word, when you engage in intercession against spiritual enemies, your work will never be in vain. You will hit the target and accomplish the very thing that arrow was sent forth to do every single time. Oh, thank You, Father, for such a great promise! Thank You, Lord Jesus!

I don't know about you, but this message ministered to me. It gave me something I didn't know I had. It was revelatory. It was transforming.

Right now, I want you to see yourself with your quiver strapped in place over your shoulder. I want you to see those marvelous, beautiful, glittering polished arrows that God is even now placing inside of your quiver. You have been tempered. You have been trained. You have been in the presence of God. You have been under His anointing. And you have paid the price to take every step He has led you to. You have been obedient, you have been submissive, and you have been teachable. Therefore, God is even now increasing the arrows in your quiver. Get ready to use them.

These are not toys. There are rubber arrows for children to play with, but these are serious weapons. Most modern arrows no longer have real feathers on them, but yours do. These are arrows

SEE YOURSELF WITH YOUR QUIVER STRAPPED IN PLACE OVER YOUR SHOULDER AND SEE THOSE MARVELOUS, BEAUTIFUL, GLITTERING POLISHED ARROWS THAT GOD IS EVEN NOW PLACING INSIDE OF YOUR QUIVER!

of antiquity, and not only are they beautiful (they are dressed with the finest of feathers and have glittering polished tips), but they are also powerful and effective.

Next, we're going to see what all of this means. I hope you are excited. I am.

The Arrow of the Double Portion

For I have bent Judah for Myself as My bow, filled the bow with Ephraim as My arrow, and will stir up your sons, O Zion, against your sons, O Greece, and will make you [Israel] as the sword of a mighty man.   Zechariah 9:13

How will God fulfill all that He spoke in Chapter 2, bringing hope and prosperity back to His people? He will do it through Zechariah 9:13. He is about to shoot forth the arrow of the Lord, bringing about His victory for you.

He said, *"For I have bent Judah for Myself as My bow."* God is the Great Archer, and we are arrows in His quiver. He will take us out, at the time of His choosing, and put us in His bow. Then, He will pull back the string of the bow and launch us with force.

For some time now, I have been in the quiver of God, but now He has taken me out to shoot me forth. In the meantime, I am using the arrows God has given me to hit every enemy that tries to come against me. It's like a double dip, a double anointing, with double power.

I firmly believe that what God is doing in the earth will go far beyond the double portion. We are now in the season of the MEGA, and that means that you will do even greater exploits!

MEGA-works speaks of the greater works. Greater than what? Greater than those done by the people who have gone before you. Your anointing will be insurmountable.

Please understand what I'm saying here. There have been many significant servants of God who have gone before us, but when we step into position in the season of the MEGA, we will do greater things than those who have gone before us. I didn't make this up; this is a true definition for the biblical word *mega*.

Now, back to Zechariah 9:13. What is God saying here? *"I have bent Judah for Myself as My bow."* God bent Judah for His own purposes.

The Hebrew word translated here as *bent* was used to refer to the attitude of a child. If a child was not *bent*, it meant that he or she was not pliable or teachable. Don't be stiff. Let God bend you. Become pliable in His hands.

THERE HAVE BEEN
MANY SIGNIFICANT
SERVANTS OF GOD WHO
HAVE GONE BEFORE
US, BUT WHEN WE STEP
INTO POSITION IN THE
SEASON OF THE MEGA,
WE WILL DO GREATER
THINGS THAN THOSE
WHO HAVE GONE BEFORE
US!

Because Judah was pliable, God was able to bend him and make him into a bow in His hands for doing warfare. How many know that if you are stiffnecked, God can't use you? You have to be bent, teachable, changeable, moveable.

Please don't misunderstand. This doesn't give us a license to physically harm our children. Instead of molding them, some parents permanently damage them. You being a tyrant over them will not help them to be properly formed or fashioned or to operate in the proper way.

God's bending is gentle and loving. He knows just how to bend us so that we don't break. We have been bent in a godly way, and we must bend others in that same godly way.

Look at this verse again. There is so much here to understand:

For I have bent Judah for Myself as My bow, filled the bow with Ephraim as My arrow, and will stir up your sons, O Zion, against your sons, O Greece, and will make you [Israel] as the sword of a mighty man. Zechariah 9:13

"I have bent Judah for Myself as My bow."
Isn't it beautiful how that starts out! Then, look where it is going. I love this passage:

The Arrow of the Double Portion

I have ... filled the bow with Ephraim as my arrow.

We know that Judah means praise, so praise and worship are God's weapons of choice. He had a bow to fight with, and that bow was praise and worship.

The prophet Hosea said:

Judah shall plow.   Hosea 19:11

When Judah plows, the presence of God follows. This means that when we praise God, it breaks up the hardened ground of our hearts, and then we are able to worship Him with a softened heart, and His presence comes.

When Jesus walked the earth, His disciples saw Him do many miracles. At one point, after He had fed a multitude, He said to them the same evening: "You just saw me take five loaves and multiply it to feed five thousand, and already your heart is hardened?" (see Mark 8:14-21).

Not only has God taken Judah as His bow; He has taken Ephraim as His arrow. Ephraim means "double portion." The Lord is using Judah as the means to shoot forth the double anointing. Indeed, He will go beyond even the double

THIS CHOSEN BOW WITH THIS CHOSEN ARROW WILL GO BEYOND AND BEYOND AND BEYOND BECAUSE WE ARE IN THE SEASON OF THE MEGA!

anointing. What He does will also go beyond the triple anointing. This chosen bow with this chosen arrow will go beyond and beyond and beyond because we are in the season of the MEGA. God is shooting the double portion, Ephraim, through the instrument of praise, Judah, His bow.

What did it all mean back then? *"I bent Judah as My bow. I filled the bow with Ephraim as My arrow, and I will stir up your sons, O Zion, against your sons, O priests, and make you, Israel, as a sword of mighty men."* God was saying that He was about to destroy the enemies of Israel, and we are spiritual Israel. We are Mount Zion. You are the City of the Most High God, and God is about to defeat your enemies.

The following verse declares:

> *The LORD shall be seen over them and his arrows shall go forth as the lightning.*

Lightning always represents the Word of God and revelation, and this scriptures states that His Word, His arrows, will be *"as ... lightening."*

> *The LORD shall be seen over them and his arrows shall go forth as the lightning and the LORD GOD*

will blow the trumpet and will go forth and the windstorms of the south and the LORD of hosts shall defend and protect them.

Zechariah 9:14-15

The Lord Himself will defend and protect you. Praise God!

And they shall devour and they shall tread on [their fallen enemies] as on slingstones [that have been missed their aim], and they shall drink [of victory] and be noisy and turbulent as from wine and become full like bowls [used to catch the sacrificial blood], like the corners of the [sacrificial] altar. And the LORD their God will save them on that day as the flock of his people for they will be as the precious jewels of a crown, lifted high over and shining glitteringly upon His land.

Zechariah 9:15-16

What does it say again? I think that bears repeating:

And the LORD their God will save them on that day as the flock of His people. For they shall be as the precious jewels of a crown lifted high over and shining glitteringly upon His land.

40

AND THE LORD THEIR
GOD WILL SAVE THEM ON
THAT DAY AS THE FLOCK
OF HIS PEOPLE FOR THEY
WILL BE AS PRECIOUS
JEWELS OF A CROWN,
LIFTED HIGH OVER AND
SHINING GLITTERINGLY
UPON HIS LAND!

How beautiful! And how powerful! What more needs to be said?

CHAPTER 3

The Making of an Arrow

For I am fearful that somehow or other I may come and find you not as I desire to find you, and that you may find me too not as you want to find me—that perhaps there may be factions (quarreling), jealousy, temper (wrath, intrigues, rivalry, divided loyalties), selfishness, whispering, gossip, arrogance (self-assertion), and disorder among you. 2 Corinthians 12:20

In this chapter, I want to discuss how an arrow is made. It requires a process that we need to be aware of, for as the arrows of the Lord, we will surely pass through a similar process of preparation.

The Choosing of the Shaft

Until recent times, arrows were always made from either tree branches or reeds growing in the water. Since we know tree branches best, let's talk about them and what is needed to get them from the tree to the quiver.

Picture a tree branch before you. Is it perfectly formed? And what does a branch normally have on it? The answer, of course, is that rarely is a tree branch ever perfectly formed in nature, and most tree branches are covered with stems and their corresponding leaves. All of that has to come off.

So, what has to happen first to a prospective arrow? Since we are the arrows of the Lord, it is an important question. Whatever is done to branches to make them into arrows is what the Lord does to us to make us arrows in His quiver. It's like a double-edged sword because not only are you the arrow of the Lord, but God is offering you arrows to send forth in Jesus' name, whether in warfare or in the teaching of the Word of God.

The Pruning Process

All branches must be pruned if they are to become effective arrows, and none of us likes to be pruned. In one of my meetings, I asked, "How many of you like to be pruned?" and several of those present raised their hands and said, "Yes." I think they must have had another type of pruning

RARELY IS A TREE BRANCH EVER PERFECTLY FORMED IN NATURE, AND MOST TREE BRANCHES ARE COVERED WITH STEMS AND THEIR CORRESPONDING LEAVES. ALL OF THAT HAS TO COME OFF TO MAKE A PERFECT SHAFT OF AN ARROW!

in mind. When you are being pruned, it is one of the most painful experiences. Pruning cuts back things that have become a part of you but will not help you to meet God's requirements.

In pruning, God strips you and cuts you back. He does this with great love and with great purpose in mind. We know intellectually that there is something greater on the other side of our pruning. Indeed, pruning will cause us to flourish, to be more powerful, to have a greater anointing and a greater ministry and to walk with greater power. This is invariably what happens when God cuts back on the "stuff" that we need to be cleansed of.

But most of us will probably never welcome such pruning. We always dread it when we know that God is about to prune us. We say, "Oh no, God! No, Lord! Please don't do this to me!"

Sometimes, when the pruning is severe, we feel that we have been cut to the bone, and we ask, "Why, Lord? For what purpose? How could this be love?" In order to make a fine arrow, a branch must be pruned. That's just part of the process. You could never take a raw branch as it is and stick it in a quiver. It wouldn't work. It could never hit a target.

Some might insist on trying it in a bow, but that arrow will not go forth with power. It could not accomplish anything of lasting value. To become an effective arrow, first a branch must be pruned.

The Sanding Process

Next, there is a sanding process. Once the pruning is complete, the artisan now begins to sand away the remaining imperfections. If you are in God, He sands away the sin, sands away at the heart issues, sands away at the mind issues, sands away at the fear issues. He will sand that arrow until it is well polished.

In the natural, what does sin do? It causes you to miss the mark. In fact, that is one of the biblical definitions of sin. The Hebrew word translated into English as *sin* is *chet,* and it means "to miss the mark." If the sin nature is operating in us, we will not be able to hit the target. We will miss the mark. That's why we have to go through the sanding process.

To hit the target (which is the opposite of missing the mark) was conveyed by the Hebrew word *yarah. Yarah* was connected to the Torah, and the Torah was the original Word of God, the first five books of our Old Testament. These books contained the Law. The Law was written for our instruction, and in it God said, "This is what you

IN ORDER TO HIT THE TARGET, YOU MUST ARM YOURSELF WITH THE WORD OF GOD AND LEARN TO OBEY THE INSTRUCTIONS OF THE LORD!

will do, and this is what you will *not* do." To miss the mark is to sin against God and His Word.

There is *chet* on the inside of every one of us that needs to be sanded out. Isn't it interesting that the meaning of sin is "to miss the mark," a phrase originating with archery itself? I think that's awesome. If we choose to be free of *chet* (sin) and strive not to miss the mark but rather embrace *yarah* (what God says we are to do or not to do), we can hit the mark every time.

But in order to hit the target, you must arm yourself with the Word of God and learn to obey the instructions of the Lord. This is a process, and when it is completed, you will be a polished arrow in the Lord's hands.

Paul wrote to the Corinthian believers of the first century:

> *For I am fearful that somehow or other I may come and find you not as I desire to find you, and that you may find me too not as you want to find me — that perhaps there may be factions (quarreling), jealousy, temper (wrath, intrigues, rivalry, divided loyalties), selfishness, whispering, gossip, arrogance (self-assertion), and disorder among you.*
>
> 2 Corinthians 12:20

What was Paul saying? That he was concerned that he might show up in Corinth (or Rome, Ephesus, Thessalonica, Galatia or any of the other churches he had established), and find the young believers there not being what they were suppose to be and not doing what they were supposed to do.

On the flip side of that, he was also concerned that one of those believers might show up where he was and find *him* not being what he was supposed to be or doing what he was suppose to do.

Paul went on to say:

Perhaps there may be factions.

We need to guard ourselves that there be no factions among us, no quarrellings, and no jealousies. Jealousy is a terrible thing. So, if you have jealousy in your heart, know that God is nowhere near you. That is one spirit that He cannot stand, and so He keeps His distance from it.

Paul's concern was that there would be quarreling and factions and that God's people would, therefore, be divided. Oh, God no! We rebuke that spirit in Jesus' name.

Paul went on to mention *"tempers, wrath, rivalries, divided loyalties, selfishness, gossiping, arrogance,*

WE NEED TO GUARD
OURSELVES THAT THERE
BE NO FACTIONS AMONG
US, NO QUARRELLINGS,
AND NO JEALOUSIES!

self-assertion and disorder among you." I charge you by the Spirit of God, Do not allow these things to enter in. Get it all sanded off so that you can be an arrow in the quiver of the Lord and when He pulls you out at the appropriate moment, you will be useful in His hands. Until then, allow Him to continue to sand you.

I wish I could give you purity of heart, but I can't. Each of us has to deal with our own minds, our own thoughts, and our own emotions, that the purity of Jesus Christ will be deposited in us and our motives be purified. Then we will no longer be prideful or arrogant.

When you get excited about the things the Lord is doing, some might mistake that as you being prideful or arrogant. It's not. I get excited about the things of God, and there's nothing wrong with that.

Pride and arrogance do exist, and Paul warned us not to allow them to hinder us. We must uproot every work of darkness around us and refuse to give them place in us so that we can remain as effective arrows in the quiver of the Lord.

Make a decision to submit willingly to the sanding process. An arrow, in order to be highly effective, must be well polished, free of debris, and with no rough places, no disjointedness, but fully smooth and free of every hindrance. Don't resist the process. Such an arrow will fly swiftly and hit its mark in a powerful fashion, doing maximum damage.

Use wisely the arrows God has placed in your quiver, and be an effective arrow in His quiver.

> *[I am fearful] that when I come again, my God may humiliate and humble me in your regard, and that I may have to sorrow over many of those who sinned before and have not repented of the impurity, sexual vice, and sensuality which they formerly practiced.* 2 Corinthians 12:21

Paul went on to say that he was fearful that when he came to them again, God would humble him among them, and he would have to mourn for many who had sinned and failed to repent of their uncleanness, fornication or lewdness which they had practiced.

The Fletching Process

First comes the pruning, next comes the sanding and then comes what is called "the fletching." This is when the feathers are attached.

Sometime in antiquity a warrior discovered that if feathers were attached to his arrows, they

THE FEATHERS ON AN ARROW ARE SYMBOLIC OF THE HOLY SPIRIT. HE IS THE ONE WHO GUIDES US TO THE PROPER TARGET AND CAUSES US TO HIT THE MARK!

would stabilize the shaft in flight. Then, through experimentation, he discovered that if the feathers were too tight, the arrow would veer off course in one direction. They had to be just right.

To us, the feathers on an arrow are symbolic of the Holy Spirit. He is the One who guides us to the proper target and causes us to hit the mark. When you are preaching the Word of God, it is the Holy Spirit speaking through you that will bring the arrow home to the heart of the listeners. Without those feathers, the arrow is unstable.

These day, when you go to buy an arrow, the fletching (and most everything else about the arrow) is synthetic, something man-made. I initially thought that I would purchase some real feathered arrows and give one to each of our people in a meeting here in Baton Rouge, but when I went looking for them, I was surprised to learn that they are no longer available. Modern arrows are made of modern materials, and, even then, they are not cheap. An arrow is the result of many processes that all take time and push up the cost. A good arrow will cost you, but you get what you pay for.

The fletching of an arrow was important, for it determined how well it would do in flight and whether or not it could hit its mark. Those feathers produced and controlled the flight of the arrow and gave it its power, carrying the arrow swiftly to its target.

If those feathers were too stiff, the arrow would move off to the left side and miss the mark. If the arrow was too flexible or the feathers had been attached too loosely, the arrow would veer off to the right and again miss the target.

Those feathers had to be precisely placed on the arrow, so the craftsman making the arrow would use feathers from the same bird and even from the same side of the same bird. The feathers used in fletching were not just plucked from any and every bird. Since the feathers had to be completely balanced, this was how they accomplished that balance.

Everything about an arrow had to be completely balanced. The shaft itself could not be either too stiff or too flexible. It all had to be done in such a way that the archer could easily fit his arrow into the bow. You and I are molded so that we can operate smoothly in the Holy Ghost. He is our feathers.

As the feathers were attached, care had to be taken that they perfectly balanced. You could have a smooth polished arrow shaft, but if the feathers had been placed on it incorrectly (if the Holy Spirit is not operating properly in your life), then that

YOU AND I ARE MOLDED
SO THAT WE CAN
OPERATE SMOOTHLY IN
THE HOLY GHOST. HE IS
OUR FEATHERS!

arrow would miss the mark, and we can't afford for that to be the case with us.

The Cresting Process

The next process in the making of an arrow was called the cresting. Cresting was basically decorating, but it served a practical purpose as well. It let everyone know who an arrow belonged to.

God is decorating you, marking you, cresting you. Crowning is a similar thing. It marks someone as royal, and God is marking His people today. He is placing His seal upon you so that when you are shot forth, you will be recognized as one of His own.

Another definition of cresting is this: "an ornamental decoration at the ridge of a roof or a top of a wall or screen." Again, this is decoration, and God is decorating you. He is hand-painting you. He wants other people to know that you belong to Him and that what you do is because of Him. He wants you to be identified as His. You have been marked by the hand of God. You belong to the King of Glory, and so whenever you are shot forth, His mark will be upon you for all to see.

Jesus said:

By this shall all [men] know that you are My disciples, if you love one another [if you keep on showing love among yourselves].   John 13:35

Our markings are markings of love, and others should recognize us because of these markings. They will know us by our love for one another.

In olden times, slaves were marked with something that identified them as belonging to their masters. Sometimes, we know, it was a mark in their ears. Whatever it was, it let everyone know who they belonged to.

Paul wrote:

But now since you have been set free from sin and have become the slaves of God, you have your present reward in holiness and its end is eternal life.   Romans 6:22

For he who as a slave was summoned in [to union with] the Lord is a freedman of the Lord, just so he who was free when he was called is a bond servant of Christ (the Messiah).

1 Corinthians 7:22

Paul identified himself as a bond slave, or bond servant, permanently marked for the Kingdom

DON'T GET UPSET
WHEN YOU FIND THAT
GOD IS PRUNING
YOU, SANDING YOU,
FLETCHING YOU OR
CRESTING YOU. HE IS
DOING IT ALL BECAUSE
HE LOVES YOU SO
MUCH AND SEES IN YOU
THE POTENTIAL FOR
GREATNESS!

(see Romans 1:1, 1 Corinthians 7:9 and 9:19 and Galatians 1:10). We are told that the ancients stood a slave who had been recently purchased against a tree, took an awl and hammer, and made a permanent mark in their ear to show everyone that they were their owner. These slaves were then known as bond slaves. We choose to become bondslaves to Christ, and we are marked, crested if you will, by Him and for Him.

Don't get upset when you find that God is pruning you, sanding you, fletching you or cresting you. He is doing it all because He loves you so much and sees in you the potential for greatness. Rejoice when He marks you as His, cresting you for His glory, placing on you the seal of His anointing. From that moment onward, the world will identify you as belonging to the King of Glory. What could be more wonderful?

CHAPTER 4

The Kairos of a Bow

Desire without knowledge is not good, and to be overhasty is to sin and miss the mark.

Proverbs 19:2

I have taught much on the *kairos* of God, so I will not repeat all of that here, but in archery, there is also a part of the bow that is known as the *kairos*, and it is important. The *kairos* of the bow is a small opening that helps the archer aim his arrow well. When properly placed in the *kairos* opening, an arrow will always hit its mark.

If an arrow is not set properly in the *kairos*, it will often veer to the right or left or even fall far short of its target. When the *kairos* is used, the arrow will not only hit the target. It will hit the target with great force.

Have you ever placed an arrow on top your finger to shoot it? For me, it usually just fell to the ground in front of me. It had no power and definitely did not hit the target. The result was not only defeat but also humiliation. When you place the arrow in the *kairos* opening and shoot it forth, it not only has greater power, but it also hits the mark.

Now, what is a *kairos*? In Greek *kairos* is a term used to denote time. There is the *chronos*, the chronological time, and there is the *kairos*, a designated moment in time that God has set apart to do something strategic. In that *kairos* moment, Heaven comes to earth, and everything around you is pregnant with possibilities.

That is also true of the arrow when it gets placed in the *kairos* of the bow. In that moment, the arrow is where God created it to be, and it can go forth in might to hit its intended target. If it does not get properly aligned in the *kairos*, there is no guarantee of victory. That arrow may well miss the mark.

When you pull an arrow out of your quiver and mount it on that bow, making sure that it is properly aligned in the *kairos* opening, and if that arrow is well polished and has gone through the pruning and sanding processes, you can be assured that when you pull back the bow and release that arrow, it will hit the desired target

IN THAT MOMENT,
THE ARROW IS WHERE
GOD CREATED IT TO BE,
AND IT CAN GO FORTH
IN MIGHT TO HIT ITS
INTENDED TARGET!

with force. It will not miss the mark, and God will be pleased.

The Arrow of Praise

Why are you cast down, O my inner self? And why should you moan over me and be disquieted within me? Hope in God and wait expectantly for Him, for I shall yet praise Him, my Help and my God.   Psalm 42:5

Are you excited to be an arrow in God's quiver? Are you excited for God to give you your own beautiful arrows to shoot? He has given you a quiver. If you didn't know that until now, then right now, in the Spirit realm, you are gaining knowledge of this fact. When you have knowledge of something, then you can receive it. When you have the knowledge of a thing, then that thing belongs to you.

You are even now gaining knowledge of the fact that God is giving you a quiver. And, now, one by one, He will begin to fill your quiver with arrows. They will be pruned, they will be sanded,

67

they will be polished. They will be ready to go forth through that *kairos* opening. These arrows are effective and will go forth speedily and hit their intended target with great power.

In Psalm 42:5, David was speaking to himself. He had been in a rather depressed state and was hungry for change. In the first verse of that psalm, he said:

As the hart pants and longs for the water brooks, so I pant and long for You, O God.

Psalm 42:1

David was thirsty for the things of God, and nothing of this world could satisfy him. He was so hungry that he was panting like a hart, a deer, that was searching through the forest for a brook to drink from.

My inner self thirsts for God, for the living God. When shall I come and behold the face of God? My tears have been my food day and night, while men say to me all day long, Where is your God?

Psalm 42:2-3

Have you ever been there? David's tears had become his food, and this was true both day and

AS THE HART PANTS
AND LONGS FOR THE
WATER BROOKS, SO I
PANT AND LONG FOR
YOU, O GOD!

night. People around him were asking, "Where is your God?" That's pretty bad, but all of us go through it at one point or another. "Where is your God?" Then David remembered something:

> *These things I [earnestly] remember and pour myself out within me: how I went slowly before the throng and led them in procession to the house of God [like a bandmaster before his band, timing the steps to the sound of music and the chant of song], with the voice of shouting and praise, a throng keeping festival.*
>
> Psalm 42:4

David remembered a better day, one in which he had led the people of Israel as a great drum major. He held the baton in his hand, and behind him came the many dancers and musicians. There was rejoicing and revelry. It was a better time.

The people were all dressed in their beautiful garments, the priests in their priestly attire, and they all formed a mighty procession to the House of God. And David was their leader.

Up to the gates they all marched together, singing and rejoicing, and on up they went to the holy places of the Tabernacle. What a sight it must have been! David remembered it well.

Today you and I have become God's Tabernacle without walls, as we bring in Davidic worship to our homes and places of business. No longer is there a Tabernacle that is closed off to us. We can enter freely, worship freely and encounter God freely.

In David's case, the sides of the tent were thrown open, and in came this great procession of rejoicing priests and everyday worshippers, and together they came into the presence of the Lord. What a memory that was!

But David was not living in the past; he was hungry in the present. His present reality was that tears had become his food day and night. That was what he ate because of the sorrows he was currently passing through. He was in a very depressed state, a very bad condition. But remembering those better times caused David to shake himself and ask himself an important question:

> *Why are you cast down, O my inner self? And why should you moan over me and be disquieted within me?* Psalm 42:5a

This phrase *cast down* refers to a depression that is uncontrolled. You might feel an oppression

IN THE MIDST
OF THIS TERRIBLE
DEPRESSION, DAVID'S
SOUL COULD STILL
WAIT EXPECTANTLY
BEFORE GOD BECAUSE
HE REMEMBERED BETTER
TIMES AND KNEW WHAT
GOD COULD DO!

from the enemy once in a while, but this was something very different. This was a deep depression, and David seemed to have no control over it. It was uncontrolled and uncontrollable.

Still, David had hope:

> *Hope in God and wait expectantly for Him, for I shall yet praise Him, my Help and my God.*
> Psalm 42:5b

In the midst of this terrible depression, David's soul could still wait expectantly before God because he remembered better times and knew what God could do.

Why should he expect any relief? In that first part of the passage, he had said, *"And why should you moan over me and be disquieted within me?"* This phrase, *"be disquieted within me,"* means "to wait for your countenance to change." What could make the difference in David's life? He was convinced that God's presence was about to come in, and that makes all the difference.

David knew that when the presence of the Lord came, he would be changed. His countenance would be lifted. There was something innate on the inside of him that told him to just wait. Things would change.

This word *wait* is very powerful. When Elijah was driven into the wilderness by the wicked Queen Jezebel, he came upon a broom tree and chose to sit down under it. There were several different positions he could have taken, and others might have been more profitable.

One of those positions meant "to wait." In this instance, the same word is used that we find in Isaiah 40:31:

> *But those who wait for the LORD [who expect, look for, and hope in Him] shall change and renew their strength and power; they shall lift their wings and mount up [close to God] as eagles [mount up to the sun]; they shall run and not be weary, they shall walk and not faint or become tired.*

This word *wait* does not mean just to sit in idleness, doing nothing. It refers to those who get yoked up together with God.

David was hanging by a thread, but he had a revelation and the understanding that if he waited with expectancy, something would change. His life was hanging by a thread, but he was determined to get yoked together with God.

When you get yoked together with God, a strong cord is produced. And, contrary to what most people

DAVID WAS HANGING BY A THREAD, BUT HE HAD A REVELATION AND THE UNDERSTANDING THAT IF HE WAITED WITH EXPECTANCY, SOMETHING WOULD CHANGE!

think, you will not have to wait a long time. It doesn't mean that at all.

David quieted his soul because he knew his countenance was about to change. The presence of the Almighty was about to sweep in upon him. He could wait in expectancy, being yoked up with God in the Spirit realm.

That word *wait* actually means "they shall spring forth speedily." God does not want you just waiting around season after season because He has said to wait. No, just get yoked up together with Him, and things will change.

That is what Elijah should have done. When he found himself in the wilderness under that broom tree, he should have waited on God, gotten himself yoked together with the Creator of all things and expected things to change.

So, although David was suffering from what seemed to be an uncontrollable depression, he quieted himself in the presence of God and waited expectantly for the change to come. He was sure that the presence of God was about to sweep in and change his countenance. And that would change everything.

Right now, I loose that on you, in the mighty name of Jesus. Remember this word. Let it not depart from you.

Now David's mood was changing: *"Hope in God and wait expectantly for Him, for I shall yet praise Him, my Help and my God. "*

My friend, get yoked up with God in expectation, in anticipation. He is about to deliver you out of the snare of the fowler. Say with David:

> *For I shall yet praise Him as my Help and my God.*

How powerful!

There are several different words in the Bible that are translated *praise*. This particular *praise* is translated from the Hebrew word *yadah*. This form of praise is very powerful.

Wikipedia says: *"Yadah* is a Hebrew verb with a root meaning 'to throw,' or 'the extended hand, to throw out the hand;' therefore, 'to worship with extended hand.' Eventually it also came to denote songs of praise—to lift up the voice in thanksgiving—to tell forth and confess God's greatness (e.g., Psalm 43:4). 2 Chronicles 20:19-20 is the *yadah* type of praise. The antonym is 'to bemoan by wringing of the hands.' "

Lifting your hands is almost always equivalent to a *yadah* (whether literally or figuratively), especially when listening to music. When you *yadah*

IF YOU ARE NOT OFFERING UP A SACRIFICE OF THANKSGIVING, NO MATTER WHAT THINGS LOOK LIKE IN LIFE, NO MATTER WHAT ANYONE SAYS OR DOES, YOU ARE MISSING IT!

to music, you are worshiping the image of the Creator, the Source of the music.

When I study the Word of God, I always look up the meanings of the original Hebrew and Greek words. All of my Bible study is done with three resources: the Bible (I prefer the Classic Amplified Version), a concordance (I prefer *Strong's*) and an English dictionary (I prefer *Webster's*). My sources tell me that *yadah* is a word that is older even than the Hebrew. It originated in antiquity when there were still active archers. *Yadah* means "to give thanks."

David was saying, *"For yet shall I praise You."* He was determined to thank God in the midst of his trial. Your thanksgiving to God goes all the way back to this *yadah*, and your thanksgiving to God will loose miracles over your life.

This is an important truth. If you are not offering up a sacrifice of thanksgiving, no matter what things look like in life, no matter what anyone else says or does, you are missing it. We must be declaring:

Thank You, God, that You will fulfill every prophetic word.
Thank You, God, that I am anointed.
Thank You, God, that You are bringing in the necessary finances.

Thank You, God, that You are more than enough for this situation.

Every time you thank God, it brings Him great joy and looses Him to do what you are already thanking Him for. This is an important principle in the Word of God.

David was saying, "I will thank You, O God, that my enemies will not be able to carry out their dire plans against me. I thank You, God, that my enemies will not have a victory over me." This was clearly a sacrifice of praise, and giving thanks changes your life by loosing God immediately to do what He has said He will do. He cannot lie, so start thanking Him for the victory now.

When David said, *"Be disquieted within me,"* he was saying, "Be silent, for my countenance is going to change because the presence of God is about to sweep into this place."

Then he went on to say, *"Hope in God and wait."* Again, this doesn't mean what some think, to sit around doing nothing. As I have noted, it means to get yoked up with God. When you do this, you will spring forth speedily, expecting great things from Your King.

"For I shall yet praise Him," David said. There is the *yadah,* the thanksgiving. Never forget to

EVERY TIME YOU
THANK GOD, IT BRINGS
HIM GREAT JOY AND
LOOSES HIM TO DO
WHAT YOU ARE ALREADY
THANKING HIM FOR.
THIS IS AN IMPORTANT
PRINCIPLE IN THE WORD
OF GOD!

yadah. The *yadah*s of God, His praises, will loose His blessing upon you. They will loose your provision. They will loose your anointing. They will loose everything you have need of.

When it looks like you don't have anything, when it looks like you don't have the anointing, or whatever it is in your life that seems lacking, the *yadah* of God will loose His blessings upon you. It will loose His hand to perform whatever you need in that moment.

But let's go back to what I said originally. This word *yadah* goes back to antiquity and has a root that extends back before the Hebrew use of the word. *Yadah* belonged to an ancient warlike people who were archers. This means that your praise is an arrow against your enemies. Your *yadah*, your thanksgiving, works as an arrow against those who would do you harm. Your *yadah* will shoot forth and hit your worst enemies, dealing them a death blow.

David knew this, and that is the reason he was determined to *yadah* his God. He started thanking God in the midst of his trial, and as he did, an arrow was going forth to perform everything that he had need of.

Yes, like David, I shall yet praise Him. I shall yet *yadah* the God of Creation. I shall yet thank Him, no matter if my countenance is fallen, no matter if every enemy is trying to overtake me. I have the arrow, the *yadah,* the thanksgiving, and I'm going to shoot it, and it will destroy my enemy, for my help is in my God.

If you can get these truths into your spirit, they will transform your ability to move in the things of God, propelling you forward.

CHAPTER 6

Arrows of Antiquity

*And His gifts were [varied; He Himself ap-
pointed and gave men to us] some to be apostles
(special messengers), some prophets (inspired
preachers and expounders), some evangelists
(preachers of the Gospel, traveling missionar-
ies), some pastors (shepherds of His flock) and
teachers.* Ephesians 4:11

I don't know if you realize it yet or not, but you
and I are arrows in the quiver of God. Not only
are we arrows in the quiver of God; but He has
trained us as His archers.

I am an archer, and you are an archer. You
pastors, you prophets, you evangelists, you
apostles and you teachers have a quiver full
of arrows. They are glistening, shimmering,
beautifully feathered, crested by the very hand
of God. You are marked, and His signature is
upon you.

You prophets, pastors, apostles, evangelists and teachers have your own quiver of arrows given to you by God, and He wants you to take them out and shoot them in the Spirit realm. When you do this, you will hit the mark. You will destroy the target.

Before the invention of arrows, battles among the ancients were fought in hand-to-hand combat. It was a bloody and terrible way to fight. Warriors desperately wanted to find a better way to face their enemies, and God showed them how to make bows and arrows and quivers to hold those arrows.

The first arrows of antiquity were very long and very cumbersome to use, but they transformed warfare. Now men could fight from a greater distance. They could even stand behind walls or other barriers and fire their arrows into the air above their enemy, to great effect.

Then came flaming arrows, arrows set on fire that would carry that fire to anything that could be ignited by it. This struck terror in the heart of those who had never seen it and brought great results to those who used it.

God has said:

> *For the weapons of our warfare are not carnal but are mighty through God to the pulling down of strongholds.* 2 Corinthians 10:4

YOU PROPHETS, PASTORS, APOSTLES, EVANGELISTS AND TEACHERS HAVE YOUR OWN QUIVER OF ARROWS GIVEN TO YOU BY GOD, AND HE WANTS YOU TO TAKE THEM OUT AND SHOOT THEM IN THE SPIRIT REALM!

For we wrestle not against flesh and blood, but ruling powers and despotisms in high places.

Ephesians 6:12

What exactly are we doing when we shoot an arrow in the Spirit? We are never shooting at a person. Our arrows are directed at the enemy of our souls.

Sometimes we need to be reminded of the weapons we have. Often when our enemies come against us, all that we can think about is how we are being attacked. Fights usually begin without warning, and we are taken by surprise.

This is why we have each other. When I am blindsided by an enemy attack, you can remind me of the weapons I have to fight and win, and I will do the same for you. Don't fight people. Fight the despotisms, the rulers in high places that are trying to operate through that person.

With the introduction of bows and arrows, warfare had forever changed. The exhausting hand-to-hand combat was no longer the norm. Men would now take their arrows, insert them into their bows, align them with the *kairos* and shoot them off into the air. Those who refined this technique had great success in battle.

The God of the universe has favored you and me by giving us glittering arrows, made with the most beautiful and balanced feathers. This is not a cause for pride, but a cause for rejoicing and rising to the battle before us.

Our arrows have been hand-made by God Himself. They are beautiful beyond description. They glitter because they have been polished by the hand of Almighty God, personally sanded by Him to perfection in every way.

In ancient times, when a king would come back home from battle and present himself before the people, his archers would send off a volley of arrows in his honor. When a king would go out to battle, the archers would go before him. Then, as he came back, they honored him by lifting up into the air in chorus their magnificent bows with their most magnificent arrows. Those bows were so long, so large and so grand. Now they took the most elaborate of their arrows and fired them into the air, all as a tribute to their leader's greatness. These were choice arrows with the finest of feathers, as big and massive as can be imagined, and yet they were shot into the air, all to honor a king.

In the Spirit realm, when our King shows up, we must do the same for Him. Honor Him, for He is the King of Kings and the Lord of Lords, and He is worthy of all of our praise. Expend your best praise for Him. You won't ever be sorry you did. It

HONOR HIM. HE IS THE KING OF KINGS AND THE LORD OF LORDS, AND HE IS WORTHY OF ALL OF OUR PRAISE!

will be like a multitude of arrows being shot into the air, our prayer, our adoration, our *yadah*, as the presence of our God, our King, comes before us.

CHAPTER 7

A Polished Arrow

> *Listen to me, O isles and coastlands, and hearken, you peoples from afar. The LORD has called me from the womb; from the body of my mother He has named my name. And He has made my mouth like a sharp sword; in the shadow of His hand has He hid me and made me a polished arrow; in His quiver has He kept me close and concealed me.* Isaiah 49:1-2

As a brief review, you and I are archers for God, and we have part in two quivers. The first quiver is God's, and we are arrows in His quiver. The second quiver He has given to us, and He is supplying the arrows we need to fill it. God is about to pull you out and shoot you into the nations, and you must pull out the arrows He has supplied you and use them to defeat every enemy.

The Word of God is a weapon in our quiver, and we must pull it out at the appropriate moment and use it wisely for His glory. He has promised that we will indeed hit the desired target.

It is important that when you shoot the arrows of the Lord you do it in a *kairos* moment. There are seasons in which God does special things, and you and I are right now in one of those blessed seasons. In these days Heaven and Earth are colliding with each other, as Heaven's will comes to pass here in the midst of us.

If an arrow is carefully selected, properly placed in our bow, and shot forth, it will hit the target every time. Your arrow will not fall to the ground and become fruitless. It will accomplish the goal that was intended for it.

In the *kairos* moment in which we find ourselves, God is shifting us all to a higher realm, a higher walk with Him. Because you are called and destined for the purposes of God, He can then do a quick work in your life and accomplish what pleases Him in a moment's time. God is raising up His army throughout the land, and you are a part of that great and mighty army. What a privilege!

Isaiah was speaking prophetically and he addressed his words to the people in *"isles* [islands],"and *"coastlands"* and *"people from afar"* or from foreign nations. That includes you and me. And the message was to get ready to be used

THERE ARE SEASONS
IN WHICH GOD DOES
SPECIAL THINGS, AND
YOU AND I ARE RIGHT
NOW IN ONE OF THOSE
BLESSED SEASONS!

by God. He was about to move in a new way, and He was extending to us the privilege of being a part of that move.

God has called us from our mother's womb, each of us. Our destiny was settled before the very foundations of the earth were ever laid.

God not only called us; He chose our name before we were yet formed in our mother's womb, and He destined us for purpose in the earth. Your name has meaning. Don't take it lightly.

There is more: *"He has made my mouth like a sharp sword."* Wow! That is for you too.

And why has God made your mouth *"like a sharp sword"*? So that you will speak in His *kairos* moment.

When you speak something as you are ministering to another person, bringing them out of the darkness into the Kingdom of God (or whatever else the Lord leads you to do), He is making your mouth a sharp sword. So, when you speak the Word of God, it will penetrate and bring forth a harvest of good.

Isaiah said:

In the shadow of His hand has He hid me.

If you seem to have been hidden, it is because God Himself has hidden you. But, clearly, that does not mean that He is finished with you or that He has cast you aside. To the contrary; He has made you a polished arrow, and in the right moment, you will be drawn forth to do what you were destined to accomplish.

Yes, God has hidden you for a time. That hiddenness may seem like obscurity and the withholding of many good things, but it is only temporary. In due time, you will be brought forth. In the meantime, there are things you must go through to prepare you as *"a polished arrow."* How powerful!

Yes, you have to go through all of the necessary processes. Yes, you must be stripped and pruned. Did you think that God would place an unpruned branch with all of its attached twigs and leaves in His quiver. Never!

Yes, you must be cut back so that you fit inside of God's quiver. Did you think that He would change His whole system just to accommodate you? No, you must be changed to fit His system.

Yes, you must be sanded until no imperfections remain. Did you think God would just overlook the sin in your life? He has called you to perfection, and nothing less will satisfy.

Yes, you must be fletched, and the Holy Spirit is your feathers. Those feathers must be applied just right. If they are too tight, when the arrow is sent forth, it will veer off to the left and miss the

YOU MUST BE CRESTED, MARKED AS BELONGING TO THE KING OF KINGS. HIS MARKS ON YOU ARE BEAUTIFUL, FOR ALL THE WORLD TO SEE, AND THEY BRING HIM GLORY!

target. If they are applied too loosely, the arrow will veer to the right of the target. Make sure you stay in the anointing of the Holy Ghost. Then, when you pull out a word and send it forth, it will hit the desired target with great power.

Yes, you must be crested, marked as belonging to the King of Kings. His marks on you are beautiful, for all the world to see, and they bring Him glory.

What are you when God has finished with you? You are *"a polished arrow,"* and a polished arrow is a thing of both beauty and utility. It looks good, and it is also deadly and powerful.

A polished arrow, when properly shot forth, will hit the target. Isn't that your desire in life? And, with all of its utility, a polished arrow is so very beautiful. It gleams.

The purpose of the polishing is not just for looks. That particular arrow will travel faster and farther than any arrow that has not been as well polished. A polished arrow flies speedily to its intended target, and nothing can stop it.

He has ... made me a polished arrow.

What a beautiful thing to say about the God of the Universe. He has made me. Then He has given me my own quiver and filled it with His arrows.

In His quiver has He kept me close and concealed me.

Yes, I am God's secret weapon. When He pulls me out and shoots me forth, the whole world will be surprised. In the meantime, He has kept me and concealed me. How powerful is that?

Why has God concealed us? Because it is not our time yet. The appropriate moment will come for Him to take us out and use us for His glory.

Behold, children are a heritage from the LORD, the fruit of the womb a reward. As arrows are in the hand of a warrior, so are the children of one's youth. Happy, blessed, and fortunate is the man whose quiver is filled with them! They will not be put to shame when they speak with their adversaries [in gatherings] at the [city's] gate.
                                        Psalm 127:3-5

Blessed is the couple that has a quiver full of children, and blessed is the believer who has a quiver full of God's arrows.

How about you? Do you want your quiver to be full? God says that those who have their quiver full will defeat the enemy at the gate of the city. This word *gate* also means "to resort to God for help,"

BLESSED IS THE COUPLE THAT HAS A QUIVER FULL OF CHILDREN, AND BLESSED IS THE BELIEVER WHO HAS A QUIVER FULL OF GOD'S ARROWS!

and that is what godly men and women have done throughout history.

In the long saga of Abraham and Lot, God was about to destroy Sodom and Gomorrah for the wickedness there, and Abraham seemed to be the only righteous man standing in the gap for those cities. Genesis 19 records the fact that Lot went to the city gate. Sitting at the city gate meant that he "resorted to God for help." Whether he did this with his heart or with his mouth, the Word does not say. But immediately he was under a divine visitation, and angels were there to meet him at the city gate, to assist his family as they fled from Sodom.

In your most difficult moments, you can stand in the presence of God, the King of Kings, at the gate, and He will help you. Our God always responds to those who seek Him.

As Lot sat at the city gate, "resorting to God for help," he soon saw the Angel of the Lord, coming to get him out of that place. God will never leave you nor forsake you. He will always be your Deliverer in your time of need. So turn the battle at the gate, and remain victorious.

CHAPTER 8

The Arrow of Victory

Now Elisha [previously] had become ill of the illness of which he died. And Jehoash king of Israel came down to him and wept over him and said, O my father, my father, the chariot of Israel and the horsemen of it!
And Elisha said to him, Take bow and arrows. And he took bow and arrows. And he said to the king of Israel, Put your hand upon the bow. And he put his hand upon it, and Elisha put his hands upon the king's hands.   2 Kings 13:14-16

There were two men named Joash who ruled God's people. The Hebrew name for Joash was Jehoash. Second Kings 3:10 tells us that Joash, King of Judah, was in the thirty-seventh year of his forty-year reign when another king was anointed by Elisha to rule over the northern kingdom, then known as Israel. His name was also Joash, or Jehoash in the Hebrew.

These two men reigned during a time when Israel was divided into two separate kingdoms, Israel to the north and Judah to the south. For the most part, Israel was ruled by evil kings and Judah by good kings, men who were of the seed of David. This good group of kings served God, often tearing down idols and uprooting all that was evil.

This was true of the first Joash, King of Judah. Like Hezekiah, another great revivalist, Joash went into the Temple to cleanse it of all abominations. When he first came to power, Solomon's Temple had been closed up, and there was no move of God there. No one was standing for righteousness, there was no tithe, and there was no functioning priesthood.

Joash reopened the Temple and began to cleanse it of all the abominations of idol worship. He took everything that was impure and dumped it in a place long used for this purpose. This dumping ground was located in the Kidron Valley outside of the walls of Jerusalem. [The Kidron can still be seen there today.]

Since the Kidron Valley was a place for abominations, it had often been associated with child sacrifice (which was and still is an abomination to God). The Moabites worshiped Chemosh, and

JOASH REOPENED THE TEMPLE AND BEGAN TO CLEANSE IT OF ALL THE ABOMINATIONS OF IDOL WORSHIP!

the Ammonites worshiped Molech, both gods that demanded child sacrifices.

Grieved that the Temple had long been closed, Joash threw open the doors to that sacred site and began a thorough cleansing of it, trusting that God would come and manifest His glory there once again.

Another Joash (also called Jehoash) was king over the northern kingdom for sixteen years. He was the son of Jehoahaz, an evil king, and he, too, was considered to be evil. Don't be surprised when you find many adversaries in the land. It has always been so. In many cases, the spiritual enemies they faced back then are the same ones we are dealing with right now.

Fortunately for this second Joash, he had a connection with the prophet Elisha. Elisha had anointed him to be king over Israel. Jehoash believed in God and worshiped God, even dancing before Him. But, because he allowed God's people to continue their worship of false gods, when he died, it was said of him that he had done evil in the sight of the Lord.

Elisha's great predecessor, Elijah, had anointed one of King Jehoash's predecessors, King Jehu, to be king over Israel, with the commission of picking up his sword and annihilating everything having to do with Jezebel and Ahab.

The connection this second Joash, or Jehoash, had with Elisha proved to be key to his survival. Let's look at 2 Kings 13:14-16 again:

Now Elisha [previously] had become ill of the illness of which he died. And Jehoash king of Israel came down to him and wept over him and said, O my father, my father, the chariot of Israel and the horsemen of it!
And Elisha said to him, Take bow and arrows. And he took bow and arrows. And he said to the king of Israel, Put your hand upon the bow. And he put his hand upon it, and Elisha put his hands upon the king's hands.

What a scene! King Jehoash was draped over the prophet, weeping, for he knew that the man of God was about to come up against his greatest enemy—death. Jehoash was fearful of the prophet's departure because he felt that he could never defeat his great enemies without the help of the prophet.

As Jehoash lay there weeping over Elisha, suddenly the prophet roused himself and began to extend himself to the king. In that moment of his departure from this life, Elisha would actually minister to King Jehoash:

AS THE ARROW OF
THE LORD WAS SHOT
THROUGH THE OPEN
WINDOW, FOR KING
JEHOASH IT WAS IN A
KAIROS MOMENT!

And he said to the king of Israel, Put your hand upon the bow. And he put his hand upon it, and Elisha put his hands upon the king's hands. And he said, Open the window to the east. And he opened it.

Then Elisha said, Shoot. And he shot. And he said, The LORD's arrow of victory, the arrow of victory over Syria. For you shall smite the Syrians in Aphek till you have destroyed them.

2 Kings 13:15-17

It was a very perilous time for the people of Israel. The Syrian army was about to attack the northern kingdom with the intention of annihilating God's people. The Syrians had the most brutal army that existed at that time. Their chariots were outfitted with iron scythes that rotated around the wheels, and when they came up against any opposing army, they simply mowed them down. In the natural, without God's help, the northern kingdom would be destroyed with all of its people.

As the arrow of the Lord was shot through the open window, for King Jehoash it was in a *kairos* moment. At the door of death, the prophet he dearly loved and depended on for his victories had suddenly received supernatural strength and risen to give him instructions about how to obtain a great victory. Step by step, the prophet was guiding the king in a sort of spiritual ballet:

Put your hand upon the bow.
Now, open the window to the east.
Now, shoot.

Each time the prophet uttered a command, the king responded:

And he put his hand upon it.
And he opened it.
And he shot.

The window of opportunity was being opened for the king at the prophet's command. It was a window to the east, and the king shot the arrow of victory out the window of opportunity to the east, to a place of new beginnings. In that moment, a great victory had just been prophetically declared for the nation and for King Jehoash.

Yet, verse 19 indicates that the prophet was angry. If the king had done everything he was told to do, why was the prophet angry? The Scriptures show us plainly:

STEP BY STEP, THE PROPHET WAS GUIDING THE KING IN A SORT OF SPIRITUAL BALLET!

Then he said, Take the arrows. And he took them. And he said to the king of Israel, Strike on the ground. And he struck three times and stopped.

And the man of God was angry with him and said, You should have struck five or six times; then you would have struck down Syria until you had destroyed it. But now you shall strike Syria down only three times.

2 Kings 13:18-19

The king had obeyed, striking the earth three times, but he had not obeyed fully. That is a key. He should have struck the ground more with his arrows. The prophet declared, "You shall defeat Syria three times, but had you struck the ground five times or more, you would have utterly destroyed that wicked nation."

But there was a connection here. God was not going to leave this young king defeated. He was pleading over the body of Elisha the prophet at his point of death. Perhaps it was because in those days the help of a prophet was the most powerful thing you could have. If you had the assistance of the prophetic or the assistance of the prophet in the land, you were destined for blessing. The Bible says:

The Arrow of Victory

Believe in the LORD your God and you shall be established; believe and remain steadfast to His prophets and you shall prosper.

2 Chronicles 20:20

As Jehoash obeyed each step of the procedure, Elisha's hand was there guiding him and cooperating with him. It was a two-fold effort.

When the king's hand was upon the bow, he was directed to shoot an arrow out through the east window of Elisha's house. That he shot the arrow to the east is very significant. The east is associated with holiness in the Scriptures. All godly things come from the east. It is a place of new beginnings and represents a new day.

I'm sure the window itself was prophetic. It was a "window of opportunity," opened to King Jehoash.

Personally, I think that Jehoash fully understood what God was saying through the prophet:

> *... the LORD's arrow of victory, the arrow of victory over Syria. For you shall smite the Syrians in Aphek till you have destroyed them.*

Jehoash knew that the old was coming down, and the new was about to be birthed. The arrow

GOD HAS PLACED
ARROWS OF VICTORY ON
THE INSIDE OF YOU TOO.
YOU WILL SEND FORTH
THE WORD OF GOD,
AND IT WILL PRODUCE
VICTORY FOR YOU TOO
AND ALSO FOR THE
LIVES OF THOSE YOU
WILL REACH!

Elisha told him to hold in his hand and then shoot was called *"The Lord's arrow of victory."* Wow!

God has placed arrows of victory on the inside of you too. You will send forth the Word of God, and it will produce victory for you too and also for the lives of those you will reach.

One morning, during the time the Lord was giving me these messages, I was not able to sense the presence of the Lord as I dressed for a weekly meeting. We can invoke His presence, but it is always in His hands as to when He reveals Himself and where. Then, during the actual service, the Spirit of God swept into our midst. His presence goes beyond my limited understanding, but when it comes, it seems so simple, and yet you know it is the presence of the Almighty God who has come to cloak you.

From the time I received the Holy Spirit, a prophetic anointing was upon my life, to prophesy and preach the Word of God. Little by little and year after year, the Lord shifted me into a greater measure of revelation. And God is expanding your repertoire, expanding your capabilities, expanding the operation of His Spirit within you. He is expanding you so that He might flow through you in more ways than you could ever imagine. Take *"the Lord's arrow of victory"* today.

Just as Elisha commanded King Jehoash, *"Put your hand upon the bow,"* do it now in the Spirit. As you do, you will feel the hand of Father God over yours, and the Spirit of the Most High God will be in control of your arrows.

Feel faith rising in your spirit, as the Lord Jesus Christ puts His hand into His quiver even now and prepares to take you out. He will place you into His bow and say to you, "Now, shoot."

The prophet said, *"Open the window to the east,"* and the king opened the window. Then Elisha said, *"Shoot!"* And the king shot the arrow. What was it? It was *"the LORD's arrow of victory,"* and you have the Lord's arrow of victory in your life too.

God said through Elisha, *"For you shall smite the Syrians in Aphek till you have destroyed them."* And that should have been the outcome—if Jehoash had only obeyed fully and not stopped by striking the arrow only three times.

God is ready to destroy your enemies too. Fully embrace what He places in your hands. Fully embrace the angelic hosts that He is even now loosing over your life. Let the angels of God go before you. Let them surround you, in the name of Jesus, to do the work of the Spirit.

The prophet showed the king an open window, and that speaks to us of opportunity. Your opportunity is surely coming. That word *kairos* means "an opportune moment," and you and I are right in that *kairos* time. There is a window of opportunity which is opening to you. Your opportune moment is at hand.

You cannot shoot before your window of opportunity opens, so don't try it, but get your arrow ready to shoot when the time is right. And the arrow of victory will be your portion.

CHAPTER 9

Hidden in His Quiver

Listen to me, O isles and coastlands, and hearken, you peoples from afar. The LORD has called me from the womb; from the body of my mother He has named my name. And He has made my mouth like a sharp sword; in the shadow of His hand has He hid me and made me a polished arrow; in His quiver has He kept me close and concealed me.   Isaiah 49:1-2

Listen to me! Isaiah was prophesying, and this word is for each of us, imparted to us to make us each a victor and a champion. But who was he prophesying to? *O isles and coastlands ... .* Isaiah spoke to the islands and to the *"coastlands."* And to both, he said, *"Listen to me."* And what was his message. He was saying, "You who preach and prophesy the Word of the Lord, you who have walked in the anointing of God, you great intercessors, you whose words will never fall to

119

the ground or be in vain, this word is for you. It is time for you to begin to prophesy and declare the will of God for the nations." Your words will be like an arrow hitting the target!

And to you God is saying today, "Prophesy to the coastlands. Prophesy to the United States of America. Prophesy to Canada and Mexico. Prophesy to Central and South America. Prophesy to Europe, Asia and Australia. Prophesy to the many islands of the sea." For some of you, the islands are calling. Hear their call today.

You peoples from afar ...

Next the prophet included *"you peoples from afar."* That takes in a lot of people. This tells me that he had a destiny to the nations. Isn't that what this Christian life is all about, a destiny to the nations?

The LORD has called me from the womb.

Every person reading this book was called by the Lord before the foundations of the earth were laid.

From the body of my mother He has named my name.

PROPHESY TO THE COASTLANDS. PROPHESY TO THE UNITED STATES OF AMERICA. PROPHESY TO CANADA AND MEXICO. PROPHESY TO CENTRAL AND SOUTH AMERICA. PROPHESY TO EUROPE, ASIA AND AUSTRALIA. PROPHESY TO THE MANY ISLANDS OF THE SEA!

From our mother's womb, God named us, called us and set us apart for such a time as this. Do the best thing in life. Obey the will of the Father.

He has made my mouth like a sharp sword.

The Word of God in our mouths is powerful to change lives. God has made your mouth as a sword, and that sword can pierce even to the dividing of your soul and spirit.

In the shadow of His hand has He hid me.

He's hiding you. You prophets, you intercessors, you who have voices, you who are to declare the Word of God, He has imparted a marvelous anointing and power on the inside of you, so that you can fulfill what He has called you to do in and for His Kingdom.

He has hid me, but I'm coming forth. He has hid me in the shadow of His hand.

In the shadow of His hand has He hid me and made me a polished arrow.

He has made you a polished arrow. That branch has been broken off of or cut off of a tree. It has been stripped and pruned. It has been sanded. Then, a point is created for it. Do you think someone would take a stick before it had a point on it and stick it in their quiver? For what? It would be useless. It needs a polished point. Then it can be hidden in the quiver until the precise moment when it is needed.

Why are arrows kept hidden in a quiver? That quiver is a protective covering that prevents the arrows from being bent, broken or warped, but it is also for the convenience of the archer. He has to have arrows available when he needs them. *Later* is never good enough. When he needs them, he needs them *now*.

Let me remind you: You are the arrows of the Lord, and He will not hide you for a moment longer than necessary. Placing you in His quiver is for your protection as well as His convenience. When He takes you out, that polished, beautiful tip must be in working order.

Some arrows have huge tips. They are a beautiful gray. When God places a tip on you, He knows that you will soon be needed. When He finally takes you out of His quiver and puts you into His bow, it means that He is ready to shoot you forth. Your fullness of time, your appointed hour, has come.

RELAX, YOU ARE IN
THE GRAND ARCHER'S
CONTROL. HE KNOWS
WHEN THE RIGHT
MOMENT IS TO PULL YOU
OUT AND USE YOU!

It that moment, it is too late for God to prove you. That has to be done long before this. If He places you on His bow, He must know that you will not bend or break, that you are well-balanced, and that you are ready to fly straight to the mark. In that moment, a bent or crooked arrow will not do.

If you have been stripped, sanded, hardened and had a proper tip applied, you know you are ready, and you are just jumping to get out of the quiver. You can't wait. You're sure that you can preach a word in due season. So, why are you still in the quiver? Relax, you are in the Grand Archer's control. He knows when the right moment is to pull you out and use you.

If another is now being used, don't question it. The Master knows best.

God keeps us in His quiver, waiting for the right moment, the right season, the right time to use us to shoot forth into the earth.

In His quiver, has He kept me close and concealed me.

You and I go through times when we are hidden and concealed by God. I believe that we have now stepped into a place where He has pulled back the curtain and is revealing us for all to see.

If God is holding you close and concealing you, it may be that He is still getting you ready. If that is the case, then He wants to take you out of where you've been and speed up the process to get you where you can be effective in His Kingdom, more effective than you have been until now.

You were created with something very special in mind. God Himself created you for His own purposes. It may be that during your growing-up years the enemy came in and tried to break or change God's bend on your life. Don't let him do that. God has bent you for a purpose, made you exactly the way He wants you. Some He has bent to be a prophet, some to be an intercessor and some to be a preacher or teacher. You can't boast in what you are. God bent you that way.

He knew what He was doing when He bent Judah. That southern kingdom was a most harsh and desolate area. It was barren there, and nothing much could grow. But Judah, praise and worship, shall plow, break up the hard and barren ground of our hearts, and make us pliable in the hands of the Master.

[I] will stir up your sons, O Zion, against your sons, O Greece.

YOU WERE CREATED WITH SOMETHING VERY SPECIAL IN MIND. GOD HIMSELF CREATED YOU FOR HIS OWN PURPOSES!

Greece, in this context, refers to the logic of man. More often than not, our spiritual warfare is against the logic of man, his way of thinking, the ways of this world, the ways in which the natural man thinks, and God is stirring up His sons against that carnal way of thinking. You and I need to start thinking God's thoughts. That will change everything.

Many of you who are reading this book have tried in the past to reach out to the lost and been unsuccessful. That's going to change now. There is a new and fresh anointing on your life for reaching the lost.

As a young Christian, I had a great zeal to help others be filled with the Holy Spirit. I wanted to lead every person I met into that experience. No one told me that I could not do that, and there was a special anointing upon me to speak to my parents, to speak to my sisters and to speak to my friends, and many received as a result. God knows how to do it, and He is stirring us up right now.

God is stirring up the sons and daughters of Zion to come up against the sons of Greece, the flawed logic of this world. In the days ahead, you will be able to bring them in one by one. You will be able to get them out from where they have been because of the special anointing on the inside of you. Their ears will now stand up, even when they would not listen to you before. When God's anointing goes before you, it will work something marvelous and different.

Even now God is stirring you up to come against the logic and thinking of man, and you will be able to reap a great harvest of souls for His Kingdom.

... and will make you [Israel] as the sword of a mighty man.

That's for you too. Amen!

CHAPTER 10

The Arrows of a Mighty Warrior

For behold, I will raise and cause to come up against Babylon an assembly of great nations from the north country. They will equip and set themselves against her; from there she will be taken. Their arrows will be like [both] an expert, mighty warrior and like his arrows—none [of them] will return in vain.   Jeremiah 50:9

God hates the Spirit of religion, and I hate it too because there is no power in it. Therefore, He has said, He will raise and cause to come up against Babylon an assembly of great nations. I am a part of that assemblage of nations, and you are too. God is raising us up as part of His great army in the earth.

God is raising us up against Babylon, which is the spirit of religion and the spirit of confusion, as an assembly of great nations from the north. And He says some wonderful things about us:

- That we will be equipped
- That we will set ourselves up against Babylon
- That she [Babylon] will be taken
- That your arrows will be like those of an expert and mighty warrior
- That none of them will return in vain

Babylon will come down, for your arrows will be like an expert, mighty warrior. You are champions and are of a mighty company of champions. God Himself has placed an arrow in the bow in your hand and commissioned you as archers for His Kingdom.

You may still be hidden in God's quiver, kept safe and secure there until the moment He needs you for a special purpose, until your fullness of time has come. When God eventually pulls you out, it will be much too late to prepare. You must be ready at all times. Especially right now. Your season has come, and He is about to shoot you forth.

Please understand: You will not have to sit there idle and unappreciated in God's quiver forever. Each of us has a special place in the Kingdom right now. We will each come to a point in time when we step into our fullness.

YOUR ARROWS WILL BE LIKE AN EXPERT AND MIGHTY WARRIOR!

In the meantime, God assures us that our arrows will be like those of an expert warrior. Did you know that you are an expert archer, a mighty warrior for God? He Himself has said of the arrows you shoot for Him, *"None of them shall return in vain."* Oh, I believe it, so do whatever you need to do to get ready for it! God is making your arrows those of an expert, mighty warrior.

CHAPTER 11

The Arrow of Destiny

Then Jonathan said to David, Tomorrow is the New Moon festival; and you will be missed, for your seat will be empty. On the third day you will go quickly and come to the place where you hid yourself when the matter was in hand, and remain by the stone Ezel. And I will shoot three arrows on the side of it, as though I shot at a mark.

And I will send a lad, saying, Go, find the arrows. If I expressly say to the lad, Look, the arrows are on this side of you, take them — then you are to come, for it is safe for you and there is no danger, as the LORD lives. But if I say to the youth, Look, the arrows are beyond you — then go, for the LORD has sent you away. And as touching the matter of which you and I have spoken, behold, the LORD is between you and me forever.

1 Samuel 20:18-23

Because I have spoken so much through the years, I have hundreds of message outlines. But I always want to speak a "right-on" word, the right word for the right moment. Anything else would be just another word, just another message. The day I spoke on Jonathan shooting these arrows, it was definitely a word from Heaven.

We don't always understand a revelation the first time we get it. It sometimes takes weeks, months and even years for the onion skin layers of revelation to be pulled back so that we can understand it more fully. When it finally comes, it is for the right moment, the right time and the right people.

One night, before one of my weekly meetings, I was very frustrated about the message. I even felt a little physically ill about it. The more I read the passage I had been led to read, the more sure I was that I didn't have the full comprehension of it. At first reading, it seemed to have a negative connotation, and I knew that was not what God intended.

I read and preach from the Classic Amplified Version of the Bible, but now I consulted other translations. Still the arrow seemed to be shot with a negative connotation. It went beyond its target, and seemed to go against the grain of what David

WE DON'T ALWAYS
UNDERSTAND A
REVELATION THE
FIRST TIME WE GET IT.
IT SOMETIMES TAKES
WEEKS, MONTHS AND
EVEN YEARS FOR THE
ONION SKIN LAYERS
OF REVELATION TO BE
PULLED BACK SO THAT
WE CAN UNDERSTAND IT
MORE FULLY!

wanted in that particular moment. But how many of you know that what you are seeing might be the old and that God is shooting an arrow ahead of you, to take you where you need to go—into the new?

One key to understanding this passage is to remember that David wanted to be set back in place as a captain over a thousand, where Saul had originally positioned him, but God had anointed him to be a king, not just captain over a thousand men. With that insight, my spirit began to leap at about 1 AM that morning. I had gotten it!

The Spirit of God has taken up His bow, He has removed an arrow from His quiver, He has placed it in the bow and pulled it back, and is even now shooting an arrow out ahead of you. He intends for you to go after it, for it is what God has destined for your life.

Now, I will lay a foundation for this truth, which will be leading up to the fulfillment of the scripture at the beginning of this chapter. First, let me say this: that same night I had an angelic encounter. It was not just with one angel, but with a multitude of angels. I wasn't able to see them, but I could feel their presence beginning to fill our home. One of the angels had been sent to me with the message for the next day, so it was delivered in grand style. As he spoke to me, he began to unravel the mystery behind this portion of scripture, and clarity was given where there had been no clarity before. We need to step out of this natural, or earthly, realm into the realm of Heaven, to receive Heaven's understanding and revelation.

I loose that upon you in the name of Jesus. What God is doing in your life is much bigger than anything you could ever comprehend. Let Him enlarge your understanding.

Now, let's see what was happening with Jonathan and David:

> *The next day an evil spirit from God came mightily upon Saul, and he raved [madly] in his house, while David played [the lyre] with his hand, as at other times; and there was a javelin in Saul's hand.* 1 Samuel 18:10

The spirit of Saul is a spirit that still operates in the world today. It is the spirit of jealousy. Very often a spirit of jealousy will rise up against you and try to stop your promotion. That evil spirit is willing to do anything and everything to hinder you, and will use every natural means. But no spirit can stop what God sets into motion.

THE EVIL SPIRIT THAT WAS UPON SAUL WAS MANIFESTING IN HIM LIKE A MENTAL ILLNESS. HE WAS NEARLY INSANE WITH RAGE!

The evil spirit that was upon Saul was manifesting in him like a mental illness. He was nearly insane with rage, and the only thing that would soothe him was for David to play and sing before the Lord. That always calmed his spirit.

David had already been anointed king, Saul's garment had been torn, and Samuel had declared that God had torn the kingdom from Saul's hands because of his disobedience. Samuel ripped Saul's garment, ripping the kingdom from him. All of this had already been done, and yet Saul continued to rule and reign as king.

David had been anointed by Samuel himself. That great prophet, the man over the school of the prophets, had filled his horn with fresh oil and poured it over David's head. They were on the backside of the desert, and one of David's brothers seemed to be a more logical choice for king, and yet David had been the one anointed, not his brothers.

The wording of 1 Samuel 16:13 indicates that he had been pulled out from among all of them and set apart from them for a royal purpose. He was now on a different level than the other brothers. He was to be king.

Therefore, the kingly anointing was already on David, and yet he would have to walk it out. In the meantime, he would have to fight certain enemies. At times, he would have to hide in caves, but, he was on a path that was ultimately taking him where he was destined to go.

No matter where God takes you, just keep putting one foot in front of the other and doing the will of God, and He will get you to your fullness of time and to the full purpose of what He has called you for.

What you did or performed in your yesterdays was not your ultimate destiny. It was only taking you to where you needed to be! That was not your fullness of time. It was just a vehicle to get you to where you are going.

From the time I was a child, I had an awareness of God and a call from God to work for Him, but then, in my early twenties, I was born again and two years later, filled with the Spirit. The presence of God would fill my car, and it would fill my home. One day I said, "Lord, what is this that You have called me to?" I could not yet see it or comprehend it. All I knew was that it was so overwhelming I couldn't even look at it. Even though God had given me a glimpse of it, I couldn't look at the fullness of it.

It was so overwhelming that I lay on the floor and began to weep before the Lord. Just the presence of God in that setting, in that purpose or

NO MATTER WHERE
GOD TAKES YOU, JUST
KEEP PUTTING ONE FOOT
IN FRONT OF THE OTHER
AND DOING THE WILL OF
GOD, AND HE WILL GET
YOU TO YOUR FULLNESS
OF TIME AND TO THE
FULL PURPOSE OF WHAT
HE HAS CALLED YOU FOR!

destiny, was so overwhelming to me that I could not bear to even get a glimpse of it.

You may do things along your journey. You may prophesy, teach, lay hands on the sick and see them healed and even raise the dead, but none of that is an end in itself. It is all taking you to where God is bringing you for your ultimate purpose.

You have already been anointed, but you are not yet walking in the fullness of what God has for you. An arrow has been shot out ahead of you, and God wants you to be moving toward it. That will take you where He wants to take you, not where you have thought to go yourself.

The next day an evil spirit from God came mightily upon Saul, and he raved [madly] in his house, while David played [the lyre] with his hand, as at other times; and there was a javelin in Saul's hand.

And Saul cast the javelin, for he thought, I will pin David to the wall. And David evaded him twice. Saul was afraid of David, because the LORD was with him but had departed from Saul. So Saul removed David from him and made him his commander over a thousand; and he went out and came in before the people.

1 Samuel 18:10-13

Do you remember the song the people sang about David: *"Saul has slain his thousands, and David his ten thousands?"* (1 Samuel 18:7, 21:11 and 29:5). That song was resonating throughout the land. Both men and women sang it. The people of God had come to love David and hate Saul, and that was why they sang this song.

That was the reason Saul removed David from his palace and gave him a military command. He wanted to sideline David, but God's Word says, *"he went out and came in before the people."* No king could stop what God wanted to do.

Now, look at the next verses:

David acted wisely in all his ways and succeeded, and the LORD was with him. When Saul saw how capable and successful David was, he stood in awe of him. But all Israel and Judah loved David, for he went out and came in before them.

1 Samuel 18:14-16

Now, let's skip to the next chapter:

Now Saul told Jonathan his son and all his servants that they must kill David. But Jonathan, Saul's son, delighted much in David, and he told David, Saul my father is seeking to kill you. Now

DURING A PART OF YOUR JOURNEY, YOU WILL BE HIDDEN, BUT REMEMBER THE ARROW SAFELY TUCKED AWAY IN GOD'S QUIVER WILL BE READY TO SERVE HIM IN A MOMENT'S NOTICE!

therefore, take heed to yourself in the morning, and stay in a secret place and hide yourself. And I will go out and stand beside my father in the field where you are; and I will converse with my father about you and if I learn anything, I will tell you.

And Jonathan spoke well of David to Saul his father and said to him, Let not the king sin against his servant David, for he has not sinned against you, and his deeds have been of good service to you. For he took his life in his hands and slew the Philistine, and the LORD wrought a great deliverance for all Israel; you saw it and rejoiced. Why then will you sin against innocent blood and kill David without a cause? Saul heeded Jonathan and swore, As the LORD lives, David shall not be slain. 1 Samuel 19:1-5

Jonathan advised David to hide himself, and how many of you know that, during a part of your journey, you will be hidden? Remember the arrow safely tucked away in God's quiver will be ready to serve Him in a moment's notice. In the quiver, it was safe. It would not be bent or ruined. The feathers on it would not be disturbed and be either too tight or too lose. In the moment it was needed, it would be ready.

For us to hide ourselves is part of God's plan. Even Elijah, after prophesying that there would be no rain for the next three and a half years, was not displayed in the earth. Instead, God told him to go hide himself.

Because Jonathan loved David, when he knew of his father's plot against the younger man, he felt he had to warn David. This was a strategic move on God's part. Jonathan advised David to remain hidden for the time being. When we are being hidden, it doesn't seem like we are doing anything to advance our destinies, but God knows what He is doing. We just have to trust Him.

David had already been anointed king, and he was ready to enter into his destiny. But Saul hated him and had reduced him to being a captain over a thousand men, and now this had happened. What was next? It seems to me that he was about to settle for something that was not God's highest will for him, when God spoke to him through an arrow.

David's desire to make things right with Saul had, perhaps, hindered him and caused him to be willing to settle for less. After all, Saul was Israel's first king, he had been chosen by God, and he was David's father-in-law. It may well be that the praises the people were offering David — *Saul has killed his thousands but David has slain his ten thousands*—had gone to his head and caused him to want to compromise. Being a captain over a thousand men was a pretty good position after all. But God had something greater in store for David.

> *David fled from Naioth in Ramah and came and said to Jonathan, What have I done? Of what am I guilty? What is my sin before your father, that he seeks my life?*
> *Jonathan said, God forbid! You shall not die. My father does nothing great or small but what he tells me. And why should [he] hide this thing from me? It is not so.*
> *But David replied, Your father certainly knows that I have found favor in your eyes, and he thinks, Let not Jonathan know this, lest he be grieved. But truly as the LORD lives and as your soul lives, there is but a step between me and death.*
> *Then Jonathan said to David, Whatever you desire, I will do for you.*   1 Samuel 20:1-4

The Word of God can be variously interpreted, and it can mean different things to different people. Someone else might teach this portion very differently, but this is what I believe God spoke to me from the passage.

JONATHAN DIDN'T CARE ABOUT THE RISK. HE WAS READY TO RISK ALL FOR DAVID'S SAKE. HE HAD SEEN THE KINGLY ANOINTING SHIFT FROM HIS FATHER TO HIS BROTHER-IN-LAW!

Saul had not been able to do any harm to David in Naioth because the presence of God there was too great, but now David fled again. He didn't just leave that place; he fled, running for his life because his enemy had come and now knew where he had been hiding.

David was perplexed and asked Jonathan to explain what he had done wrong, why his father was so angry with him. What was he guilty of? What sin had he done?

Jonathan was determined to help David, even risking his father's wrath. He would listen for the king's plans and relay them to David so that he could escape.

David wasn't sure this would work. After all, Saul knew that his son was very fond of David, as he had once been himself. He was part of the family. Therefore, he would surely conceal his real plans from Jonathan. He was also concerned that what Jonathan was proposing might put him at risk if his father learned about it. Jonathan, however, didn't care. He was ready to risk all for David's sake. He had seen the kingly anointing shift from his father to his brother-in-law.

This all led to the two men, Jonathan and David, cutting a covenant. They were now knitted together for all generations. Their lives became as one because this union was so powerful between them. That was when David put forth his plan:

> *David said to Jonathan, Tomorrow is the New Moon [festival], and I should not fail to sit at the table with the king; but let me go, that I may hide myself in the field till the third day at evening. If your father misses me at all, then say, David earnestly asked leave of me that he might run to Bethlehem, his city, for there is a yearly sacrifice there for all the family. If he says, All right, then it will be well with your servant; but if he is angry, then be sure that evil is determined by him. Therefore deal kindly with your servant, for you have brought [me] into a covenant of the LORD with you. But if there is guilt in me, kill me yourself; for why should you bring me to your father?*
>
> 1 Samuel 20:5-8

This brings us back to the scripture at the beginning of the chapter—1 Samuel 20:18-23. There is a two-fold message in this passage. The next day was the new moon, and it was a time for festivities. It was actually a full moon. (The Feast of the New Moon is even mentioned in the New Testament.) David would be required at Saul's

SAUL HAD NOT BEEN
ABLE TO DO ANY HARM
TO DAVID IN NAIOTH
BECAUSE THE PRESENCE
OF GOD THERE WAS TOO
GREAT!

table. The feast was a time of consecration, and every time we see a full moon we should think about that. This was what was known as a High Holy Convocation, and that was why David's presence was required. Because it was a feast, a High Holy Convocation, no one was exempt from attending. As a captain over a thousand and as a member of the family, this was David's duty.

The feast would last for two or three nights, and, more than likely, Saul would notice that David was absent. He would go to Jonathan and ask him where David was. "If so," David said, "tell him that I have gone to Bethlehem with my brothers to celebrate and offer up certain sacrifices that are required of my family. So, I have an excuse." The truth was that David was hiding in a nearby field, and he would hide himself until the evening of the third day.

I had read that passage many times and had it highlighted in my Bible, but when I read it this time, it had new meaning for me. Another onion-skin layer was being pulled back. We are a third-day people, so this teaching is for us.

David was about to hide himself in the field, and each of us has a harvest field. David was going into this harvest field to hide himself there until the third day. He, of course, was referring to the third day of the Feast of the New Moon, but that speaks prophetically to me about the day in which we are living. He would reveal himself in the evening of the third day.

Some believe in the Rapture (I, for one, do), and some believe that we are to stay here and establish God's Kingdom on Earth. But whatever you believe, it is clear that the Scriptures speak of a day being as a thousand years. We are in the third day after Jesus came to Earth, and in the evening of the third day, the Lord will return. David's words were prophetic, an indicator of the timings and movings of God in the earth.

Jonathan answered:

Jonathan said, Come, let us go into the field. So they went into the field. Jonathan said to David, The LORD, the God of Israel, be witness. When I have sounded out my father about this time tomorrow, or the third day, behold, if he is well inclined toward David, and I do not send and let you know it, the LORD do so, and much more, to Jonathan. But if it please my father to do you harm, then I will disclose it to you and send you away, that you may go in safety. And may the LORD be with you as He has been with my father. While I am still alive you shall not

WHATEVER YOU
BELIEVE, IT IS CLEAR
THAT THE SCRIPTURES
SPEAK OF A DAY BEING
AS A THOUSAND YEARS.
WE ARE IN THE THIRD
DAY AFTER JESUS CAME
TO EARTH, AND IN THE
EVENING OF THE THIRD
DAY, THE LORD WILL
RETURN!

only show me the loving-kindness of the LORD, *so that I die not, but also you shall not cut off your kindness from my house forever—no, not even when the* LORD *has cut off every enemy of David from the face of the earth. So Jonathan made a covenant with the house of David, saying, And the* LORD *will require that this covenant be kept at the hands of David's enemies.*

1 Samuel 20:11-16

On the third day, something very powerful and prophetic would take place. Here is what transpired:

On the third day you will go quickly and come to the place where you hid yourself when the matter was in hand, and remain by the stone Ezel. And I will shoot three arrows on the side of it, as though I shot at a mark. And I will send a lad, saying, Go, find the arrows. If I expressly say to the lad, Look, the arrows are on this side of you, take them—then you are to come, for it is safe for you and there is no danger, as the LORD *lives. But if I say to the youth, Look, the arrows are beyond you—then go, for the* LORD *has sent you away.*

And as touching the matter of which you and I have spoken, behold, the LORD *is between you and me forever.*

157

Behold it is well inclined to David and I do not send and let you know ... for the LORD do so much more to Jonathan ... if it pleases my father to do you harm then I will disclose it to you and send you away.   1 Samuel 20:19-23

The lad in question who helped Jonathan execute this matter was his armor-bearer. And what was unusual about all of this? It was a time of holy convocation, a time when no one went out to hunt, and neither did they target practice. It was against the spiritual laws of the kingdom. Again, Jonathan was risking his life, but he did it nonetheless for David's sake.

David was to go to a certain stone named Ezel. This meant the Stone of Departure. This wasn't a little stone. It was big enough for David to hide behind. So, on the third day he was to hide himself behind the Stone of Departure.

It was against the laws of the kingdom for a man to be using a bow and arrows on that day, but Jonathan had determined to shoot his three arrows anyway. If King Saul was not coming after David, then all three of those arrows would fall to the side of the Stone of Departure where he was hiding.

Three arrows, three nights of feasting, and on the third day he would shoot the three arrows ... Wow, something important was going on here!

ON THE THIRD DAY, SOMETHING VERY POWERFUL AND PROPHETIC WOULD TAKE PLACE!

On the second night of feasting, Saul noted David's absence and asked Jonathan where he was. Jonathan answered, "David asked to be excused because he was going to Bethlehem to offer sacrifices with his family. Since they were sacrifices that were required of him, I gave him permission to go."

By the third night, when David still had not returned, Saul was enraged and told Jonathan that he would kill David. Disappointed and full of righteousness indignation, Jonathan asked his father, "Why would you want to kill David?" And he left that place angry with his father and ready to fulfill his promise to David.

All the while, I believe, Jonathan sensed that David was thinking about going back and making peace with Saul. After all, he would still be captain over a thousand men. That, however, was not the plan that God had for him.

When it came time for Jonathan to shoot the arrow, it went beyond David. That caused me to totally forget the negatives in this story and focus on the positive. And what was that positive? God had shot an arrow out ahead of David, beyond him, and it was up to him now to go toward the Lord's arrow.

Jonathan shot the arrow, and it went beyond the stone where David was hiding. I can just imagine what David was feeling about then. Before this, he had been consumed with his loss, so much so that he was hiding for his life. He was in imminent danger of being driven into the camp of the Philistines, when all he wanted to do was faithfully serve Saul and be one of his captains over a thousand men.

But this was not what God had in store for David. God's purpose for him went beyond his current circumstances. He would have been happy to go back to the palace and continue serving Saul (if he would not kill him), but then he would have remained captain over a thousand men. God's plan was greater.

God was calling David to be king, to lead a nation, not just a thousand men. When the arrow went beyond him, his heart must have sunk. He now had to turn and leave that place, for he was at the Stone of Departure. He was not going back to where he had been. He was departing for a new place.

David was at the Stone of Departure, and all that he could think of or see was the possibility of him again being captain over a thousand men. He felt good about that, and the people loved him. They sang that wonderful song about him. He was a great captain in their eyes. But God had something else in mind for David.

OUR GOD HAS SHOT HIS ARROW OUT AHEAD OF YOU, AND THIS IS TO INDICATE WHERE YOU MUST FOLLOW. THIS IS YOUR DESTINY!

This is why the Spirit of God, through Jonathan, took that bow and arrow and shot an arrow beyond David. All that David could see at the moment was where he wanted to be, and his heart sank. But God said,"No! I am calling you to be a king. I am calling you to rule My kingdom. So you can't stay here. You have to go do what I am telling you to do!"

David did not suffer even one defeat on his journey to the palace, and you can claim the same. As you are on your journey to the palace, it may seem as if you are suffering defeat, but, in the end, there will be no defeat. God may allow you to experience temporary setbacks, but your journey is ever onward and ever upward in Jesus' name.

Our God has shot His arrow out ahead of you, and this is to indicate where you must follow. This is your destiny. This is your purpose. You are not leaving anything behind; you are moving toward something greater and fuller.

Amen!

Author Contact Page

You may contact Andy McDougal in the following ways:

AndysMinistry@gmail.com

www.facebook.com/andrea.mcdougal.3
www.facebook.com/andymcdougalministries

225-572-9844

Other Books by Andy McDougal

THE
GLORY
OF
GOD
REVEALED

The What, the Why and the How of the
Current Revival of Signs and Wonders

Andrea "Andy" McDougal

HIS WONDERS IN THE DEEP

GOD'S CALL TO THE SUPERNATURAL

Andrea "Andy" McDougal

YOUR Camels Are Coming

The Bride's Journey
to
Destiny

Andrea "Andy" McDougal

The
Power
of the
Seed

Andrea "Andy" McDougal

A Southern Lady's Tea Journey

A Legacy

Andrea "Andy" McDougal

A Southern Lady's Tea Adventures

Andrea "Andy" McDougal